POSTER BOOK

THE WORLD OF
HARRY POTTER

Harry Potter
™

POSTER BOOK

THE WORLD OF
HARRY POTTER

SCHOLASTIC INC.

New York   Toronto   London   Auckland   Sydney
Mexico City   New Delhi   Hong Kong

ISBN 978-0-545-31482-4

12 11 10 9 8 7 6 5 4 3 2 1   11 12 13 14 15 16/0

Art Direction by Rick DeMonico
Book Design by Heather Barber

Printed in China First printing, September 2011   95

CONTENTS

PART I
LIFE
AT
HOGWARTS™

STUDENT PORTRAITS

Harry Potter™

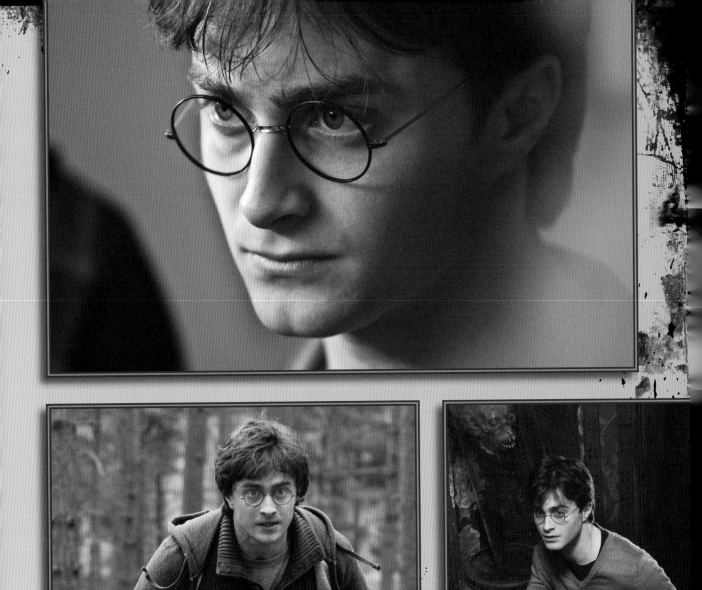

Hermione Granger™

Ron Weasley™

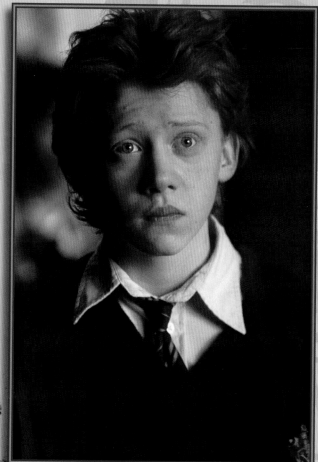

Ginny Weasley™

Fred & George Weasley

Neville Longbottom™

Seamus Finnigan

Dean Thomas

Romilda Vane

Cormac McLaggen

Lavender Brown™

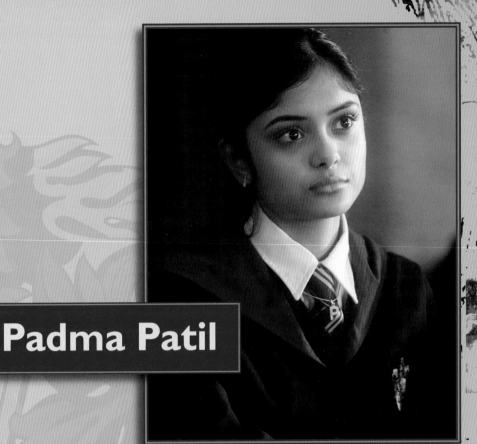

Padma Patil

Parvati Patil

Draco Malfoy™

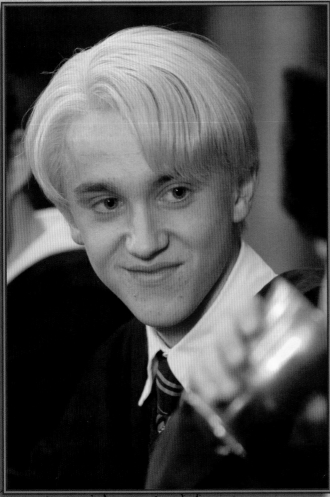

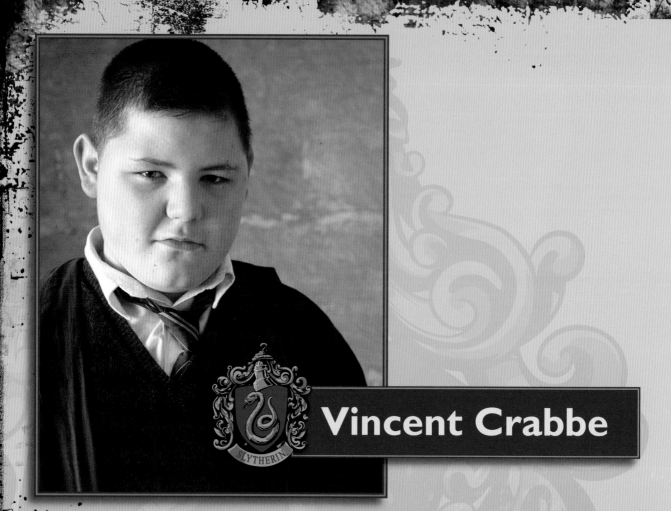

Vincent Crabbe

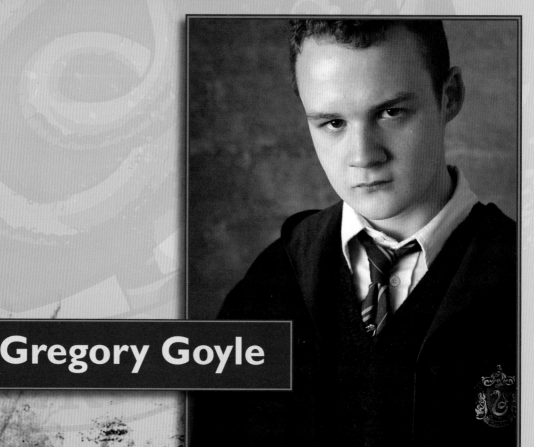

Gregory Goyle

Blaise Zabini

Cedric Diggory

Cho Chang

RAVENCLAW

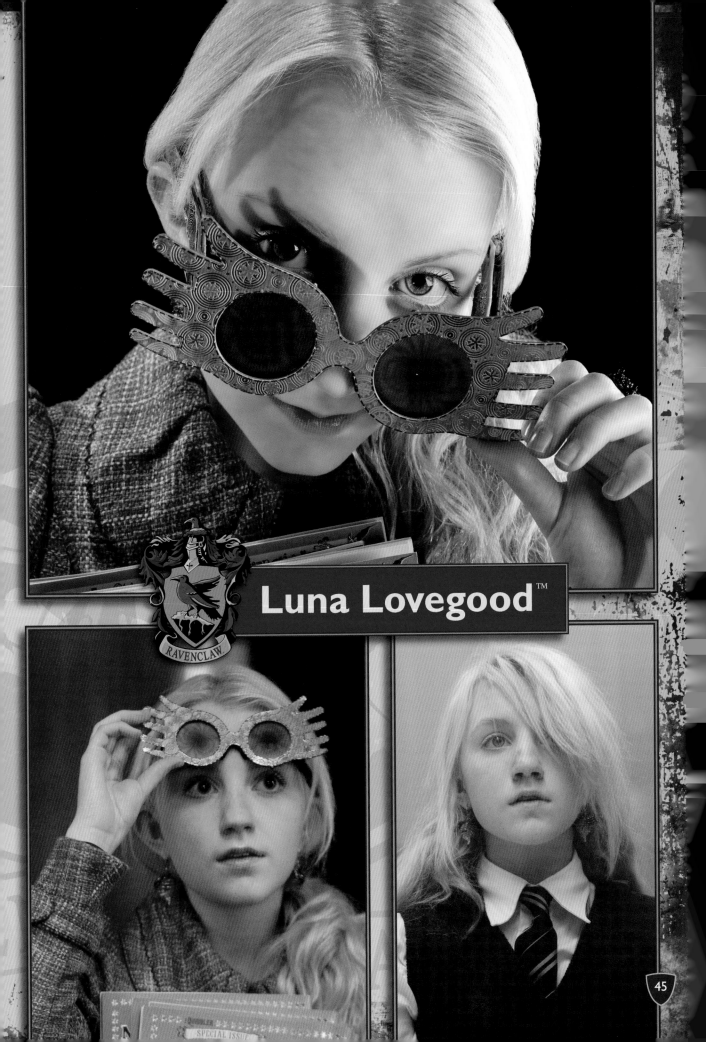

Luna Lovegood™

HOGWARTS CASTLE AND GROUNDS

Hogwarts Castle

The Fat Lady

Library

The Great Hall

The Chamber of Secrets™

Gryffindor™ common room

Corridors and staircases

Quidditch™ pitch

Potions classroom

Hospital wing

Room of Requirement

Whomping Willow

Slytherin™ common room

Owlery

Hagrid's hut

Forbidden Forest

STAFF AT
HOGWARTS™

ALBUS DUMBLEDORE™
Headmaster (Years 1-6)

MINERVA McGONAGALL™
*Deputy Headmistress, Transfiguration teacher,
Head of Gryffindor house*

RUBEUS HAGRID™
*Keeper of Keys and Grounds and
Care of Magical Creatures teacher*

SEVERUS SNAPE™
*Headmaster (Year 7), Defense Against the Dark Arts
teacher and Head of Slytherin house*

FILIUS FLITWICK
*Charms teacher and
Head of Ravenclaw house*

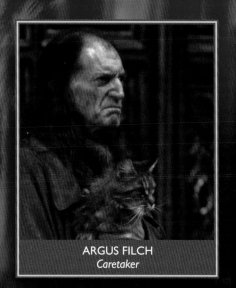

ARGUS FILCH
Caretaker

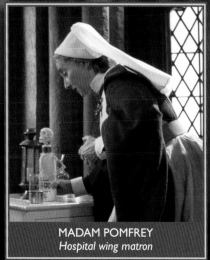

MADAM POMFREY
Hospital wing matron

SIBYLL TRELAWNEY
Divination teacher

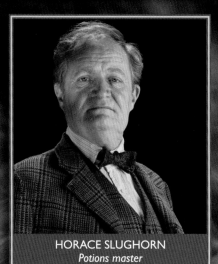

HORACE SLUGHORN
Potions master

POMONA SPROUT
*Herbology teacher and
Head of Hufflepuff house*

MADAM HOOCH
Flying teacher and Quidditch referee

DEFENSE AGAINST
THE DARK ARTS TEACHERS

QUIRINUS QUIRRELL
Year One

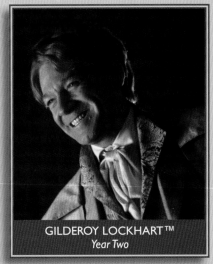
GILDEROY LOCKHART™
Year Two

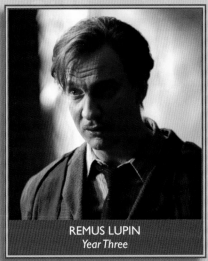
REMUS LUPIN
Year Three

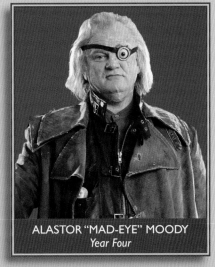
ALASTOR "MAD-EYE" MOODY
Year Four

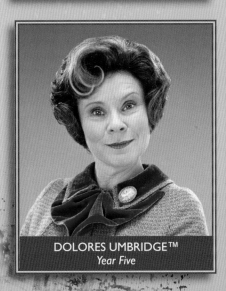
DOLORES UMBRIDGE™
Year Five

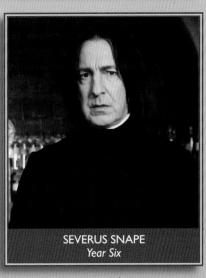
SEVERUS SNAPE
Year Six

STUDENT LIFE

DUMBLEDORE'S ARMY

THE YULE BALL

THE SLUG CLUB™

THROUGH THE YEARS

PART II
THE WIZARDING WORLD

Ministry of Magic elevator

Visitors' entrance to the Ministry of Magic

Wizengamot

DIAGON ALLEY

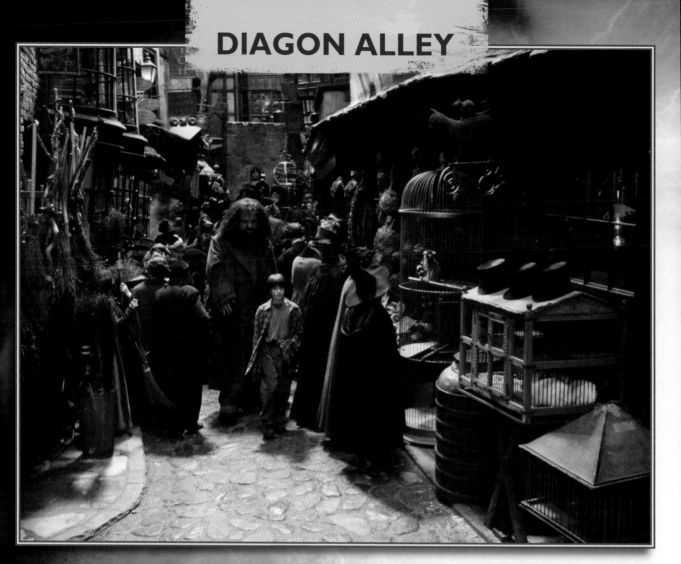

Weasleys' Wizard Wheezes

Eeylops Owl Emporium

Ollivanders

Gringotts

HOGSMEADE

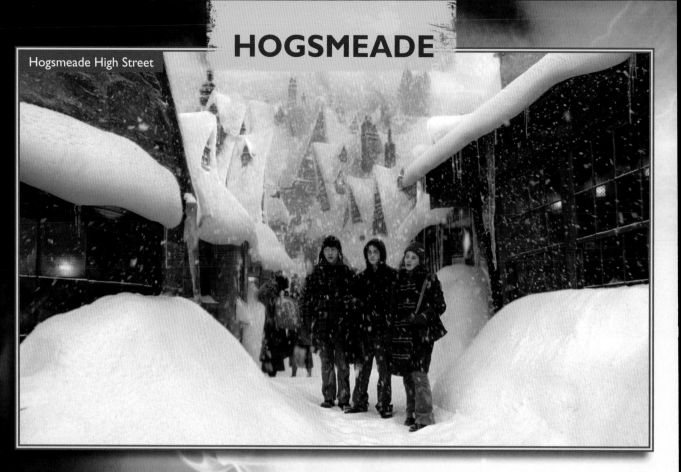

Shrieking Shack

Hog's Head

Honeydukes

MAGICAL CREATURES

Fawkes™ the phoenix

Dementor

Dobby™ the house-elf

Basilisk

Werewolf

Goblin

Thestral

Buckbeak™ the Hippogriff

Hungarian Horntail dragon

PART III

BATTLING DARK FORCES

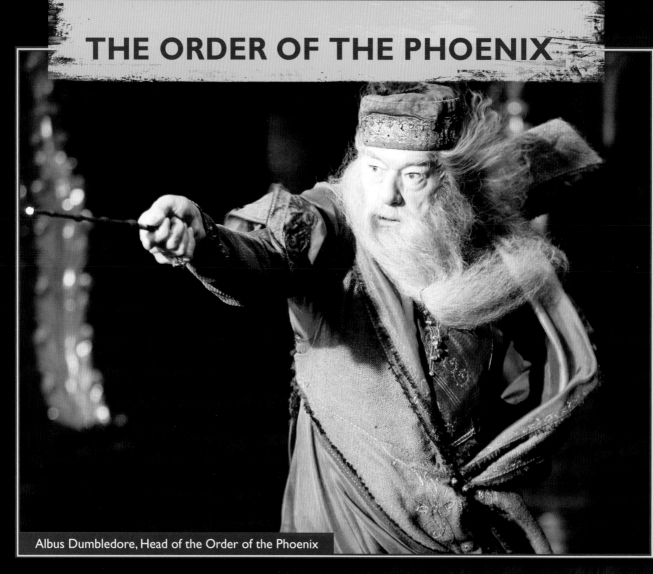

Albus Dumbledore, Head of the Order of the Phoenix

Severus Snape

Remus Lupin

Sirius Black™

Arthur Weasley

Molly Weasley

Fred and George Weasley

Bill Weasley and Fleur Delacour

Kingsley Shacklebolt

Alastor "Mad-Eye" Moody

Nymphadora Tonks™

Minerva McGonagall

VOLDEMORT AND THE DEATH EATERS

Lord Voldemort™

Bellatrix Lestrange

Lucius Malfoy

Draco Malfoy

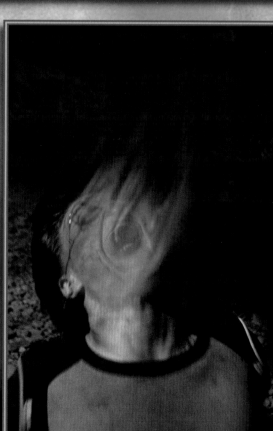

VOLDEMORT RETURNS

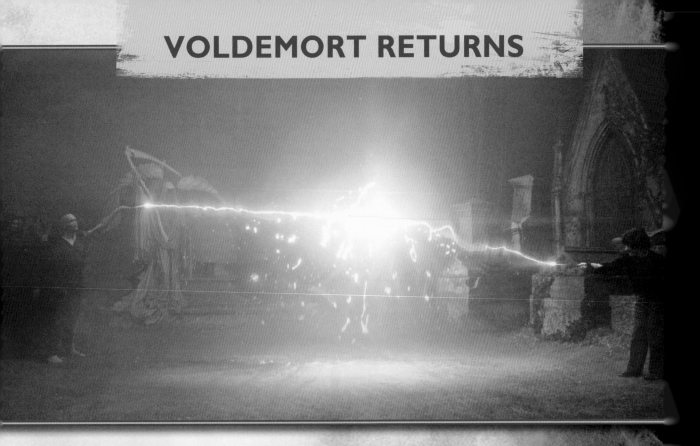

BATTLE AT THE BURROW

DEATH EATERS AT HOGWARTS

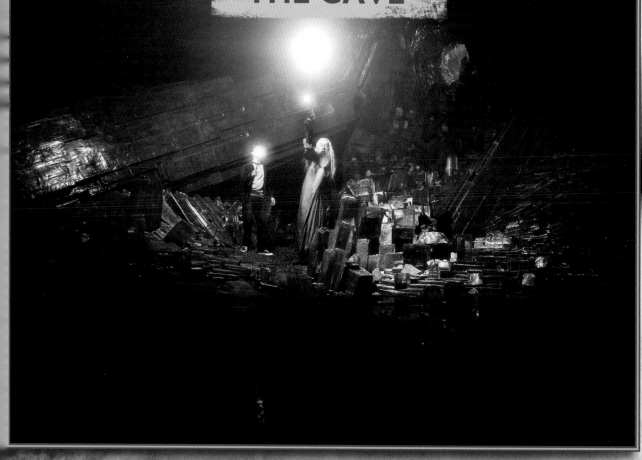

FLEEING THE SNATCHERS

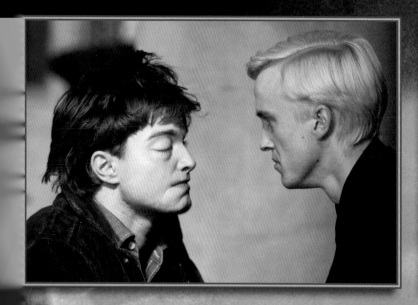

THE BATTLE OF HOGWARTS